# LIFE

## Shared thru Poetry

Life

Shared thru Poetry



Any Inquiries contact cheryl.hiller@yahoo.com

Some of the poems in this collection first appeared in Mount Shasta Bioregional Ecology Center, May 2023 newsletter; Love Unconditional, Know Your Way, We Are One and Follow the White Rabbit chapbooks and on facebook.

Cover photo credit, taken by Cheryl Lunar Wind.

First edition.

Published by Four Wild Geese Design, Mount Shasta, California 96067

ISBN 978-1-7324373-6-4

## *Preface*

Life shared thru poetry takes the reader into the thick of it. Mothers, daughters, growing up, relationships, loss--it really deals with most aspects of being human and maneuvering thru life.

This book is a collaborative effort. Again, it is my honor to facilitate this sharing of experiences and thus wisdom. We learn from our experiences, and as we share them we assist others on their journey.

Never regret your life choices---because it's all a journey of learning.

All contributors keep the rights to their writings. Much love and gratitude.

“Life is a highway, and I’m gonna ride it all night long.”

"Looking at a lake so calm that not even the wind dares to ruffle it, a liquid mirror reflecting the sky, a calm so perfect birds grow quiet before it. The place the holy fills in your soul is like that lake--the still center at the heart of who you are. Trust that deep core of untroubled hope, that peace beyond our understanding, that reminder of a home you once knew and will find again."

~Native American elder Steven Charleston

## Contents

## Palm Sunday

I'm waiting
for the sun.

No, really.
I'm sitting in my chair
looking out the window--
with my artificial light and heat,
waiting for the real.

The sun sends us
tubes of light--
like a Nova
burning bright.

Crow caws
his morning song--
"Come out, come out.
You belong."

The last hold of winter--
white sky, white ground
white roses in my room.

Living in the Shasta forest,
Lilies and Palms
are shipped in
to local stores and nurseries.

There's a place on Route 99--
where Palm meets Pine.

I hear the sun is shining there.

## Silent Places
### by Hazel Scarlett

I love still things and silent places.
The soundless, shining calm of a summer day, when even the soft wind holds its breath and all nature seems to slumber.

A still, dark pool in the canyon's curve, where the stream ceases to laugh and lies motionless, reflecting the silent shadows around it.

An empty cabin hidden deep in the quiet wood, where the birds have left their vacant nests above it, and no footfall startles its sleeping threshold.

A broken gate entwined with small wild roses, white and still and wrapped in fragrance, where old memories seem to cling, and ghosts of old home-comings.

A tiny rock-walled church, among great brooding trees that spread green arms around it, and raise still heads above it as though in wordless prayer.

A lone tree-giant high upon a barren hilltop, with gaunt boughs flung in stern and changeless posture against the contrast of a rose-flushed morning.

The deep, far blue of cloudless mountain skies and the silent, mystic brightness of moonlight on still water.

There is a golden harmony that sings from the heart of silent beauty, more deeply enthralling than the most melodious chords of sound. The song of the robin is sweet when dawn is astir with wakening voices; but when the bird sits silent on a blossomed bough, high and unmoving against the cool sky's serenity, his red breast shining in the sunlight----it is then that he creates the song unknown to sound, the music that only the beauty-loving heart may comprehend.

The throb of an organ's full solemn tones mingled with singing voices often brings a thrill of sacred joy to the listener; but when the throng has departed and the music hushed, when the pale still light of a slender moon slants through many tinted windows, to lie upon the whiteness of silent keys, and search the shadowed altar with long, transparent fingers---
then the soul of the lone worshipper seems to hear the far-off singing of angel voices, and strains of unearthly music stealing out through unfathomed space.

For the silent voice of Beauty in all created things is the love-song of God to Eternity, and only that which is eternal may hear and understand.

## **Tiny Bowl** by Cheryl & Giovanna

Background sounds bring life to food.
Good company, place to be free.
A tiny bowl filled with compassion--
Washes away a yearning heart.

Good company, place to be free.
Flowing, Cleansing heart and soul.
Washes away a yearning heart.
Longing to be loved and free.

Flowing, Cleansing heart and soul.
Holding space for all to heal.
Longing to be loved and free.
I see you and you see me.

Holding space for all to heal.
A tiny bowl filled with compassion--
I see you and you see me.
Background sounds bring life to food.

## Shadows/
## Cycle of Life
**by JahSun**

You won't see the shadows when we glow
Light shines down from above
Submit yourself to the flow
And brace yourselves
For Love

Struggle comes, and then it goes
Love is the song we all know
Stars shine bright, then they die
Such is the cycle of life

Send your prayers up to the sky
And to this Earth may she alight
A burning fire in your Soul
To return, to return us all Home

## The Light You Lit
**by Eleanor Glifort**

You spread your wings
To help us learn.
We follow your path
And take each turn,
With happy souls
And joyful hearts,
Because this is the start.
We live, we learn,
We grow and see
What it is you meant for we.
We become a light that you first lit,
Showing others
What you have shown us.
We understand,
And hope we can be
Just as good as you were,
To each and every detail.

## **Sanctuary** by Darrel Johannes

The road to Church is full of feelings,
times of loneliness, times of healing.

Sometimes expecting more than it is
leaves me empty, feeling amiss.

Seeking  a refuge from cruelty and shame,
but often there I feel the same.

Challenges and guidelines, the way explained
when all I need is simple refrain.

Refrain from study, logic and plans--
only desiring to rest safe in his hands.

Hands that hold, heal and bless
Removed from the world's mechanical mess.

The competition is there to show what we know--
the pressure is on to "grow grow grow".

Pressure cooked to perfection, where's the good in that?
Presto Saint--right out of the hat.

Good growth is slow, deliberate and right.
We yield to the spirit and give up the fight.

We fight and demand to know how it works--
Dear God please deliver us from arrogance.

Sanctuary, just the sound draws me in--
a place of mercy, compassion and kin.

A place of safety from the world's ways
a place to be just me, free from the craze.

From the craze of performance, judgment and stress
to a place of warmth, beauty and rest.

Sanctuary, not a building, address or place--
its an attitude we build with forgiveness, acceptance, and grace.

**Syllabus for Life**

Grandmother says
"Young one,
Let me give you some advice---

Look forward---
Stay Focused.

Don't worry what others are doing---
Follow your own heart whispers."

Sometimes,
the way we think is ours---
is not. So,
find your way!

Be aware--
Everyone is doing their thing---
Don't compare!

Our job is to find
Our thing.

FOMO
Fear of Missing out---

Is the grass always greener
on the other side---

Feeling sorry--
Making comparisons--
Feeling left out--

"But they have it better than me."
"No one knows the troubles
I've seen."

Honey,
that's your path--
your contract
for your soul development.

Do you realize
you chose the details?

I Am
a tight rope walker---
balance beam gymnast---
Teetering between---
Compassion and Boundaries.

What happens if I fall?

I Am following my own Syllabus.

Can't worry about
what others are doing---

No longer concerned
about what I'm missing.

I know--
I Am here for my stuff.
What's for me--
comes my way.

My map is internal.
It is my Syllabus for Life!

## All I Ever Wanted Was a Family
**by Jan Dorrell**

All I ever wanted was a family.
I longed for, lived for the day
I would have my own.

An unplanned pregnancy,
the father wanted to terminate--
Not possible.

All I ever wanted was a family.

Our daughter was born.
We stayed together
and shared the joy of bringing
four beautiful children
into the world.

Life was filled with
joy, laughter and
Yes,
sometimes tears.

Holidays with family,
were busy, special trips--
planning, sharing incredible events.

I watched in awe as my babies grew into unique,
interesting, intelligent adults.

One day,
their dad told me he no longer felt anything for me.
After 33 years together,
crushed, devastated and angered by his betrayal.
Tears, pain, hurt
and feelings of unworthiness.
I could barely breathe most of the time,
much less be a mother.

Grasping for meaning,
I made a big mistake,
Enter the sociopath finding a perfect target.

He isolated me
From my children
From my sisters
From my friends
I allowed him to destroy my life.

I lost my home.
I lost respect.

Everything of value,
stolen from me
and pawned.

I acknowledged,
I would not have my family again,
the same way.

I had to rebuild, restart.

I have two children who won't talk to me
four grandchildren I'm not allowed to see.

Debt, poverty and illness are my life.
Alone and lonely.

How can this happen when
All I ever wanted was a family?

## Feelings

In the world of flesh
it's easy to feel alone.

I appreciate my spirit guides---
I long to be with them.

Am I in the wrong place?
Wrong side of the coin?

On the spirit side---
Are they more enlightened?

I have been giving for a long time.
Tired.
Weary, I am.

"Oh, she doesn't call me, so I won't call her."
"Oh, he doesn't talk to me, so I won't talk to him."

When I see my mother's behaviors in my children---
I feel angry
Want to isolate
Shut them out.

My secret fear is that my childhood was so F-----Up
that we don't have the skills to be a co-hesive family.

My mom was not a grandmother.
My dad wasn't a grandfather.
Now, I am missing those joys.
Feeling sad.

Triggers,
bring up those feelings buried deep down.

Are we going to keep poking each others wounds?
When will it end?

Heal the wound with self love.
Accept yourself.
Be ok with your life.

Let go of the false reality.
Expectations cause pain.

Kindness Begets Kindness.

Be Yourself.
Just Be.

## Release by Damien Balderrama

Feeling my interconnection with all of life,

I peeked into the fabric of infinity and witnessed nature whispering from within.

I embraced the potential of what may never be and open to the guidance of what always was.

Tasting the elixir of Nature's breath, intoxicated with her perpetual death.

Resuscitated, again, by her endless birth.

Swimming in the womb of my own self-worth.

A worth not just mine, though perceived as such,

was fine china Divine displayed in Eternity's Hutch.

Filthy windows, open, view now clear.

A seer of the symphony I never could hear.

Fear, evaporating, like morning dew in the sun's kiss.

Limits sink into Sapphire Abyss.

Timber... Borders, cut down, fell by a lumberjack named presence.

Imagination emancipated by Authentic Essence.

The essence of me is the O, the N, the E. Effervescent luminescence bubbles up to be freed.

Passive voices perpetually echo in the cavern of psyche.

Screaming praises of parole and liberation of what might be.

Tightly, gripping, upon the illusion of identity; I release.

## The Spirit of All Life by Catherine Preus

It is so hard to live,
to know how to live in a sacred manner
Darkness and confusion reign
but underneath it all
the spirit of All Life
moves and breaks through in terrible
and wonderful truth

It is so hard to live
We are a scattered and broken people
set adrift, looking for crumbs.

Once, the whole of life was strong,
people knew how to live.
Daily life was good,
organized along sacred lines
like the bees and the ants.
People knew their sacred role.
The way was clear,
revealed to all through visions
and prayers that were the
invisible ropes that guided and
helped all on the daily path of living.

To be alive
was not so hard
as it is today
with every person alone,
each day striving to hold the faith.

For to live without the collective agreement
it is harder,
much harder,
to know how to live,
how to learn,
how to worship.

Life becomes chaotic and dark
people bicker and fight amongst themselves
only a few people survive,
living what's real in their hearts.

The poets and artists feel this the most.
Others cling desperately to their illusions of happiness.
Drink and despair and insanity flow through humanity
like a dark current sweeping
many into the gutter.

But a New Day is coming!
A New Day is here!

So it is said,
and I believe it.

We can only share our brokenness
and thus help, by healing our own wounds,
to make this new day possible,
this day which is dawning
with a terrible and wonderful
certainty, and which like the sun,
can no longer be held back.

New ways are blending with old ways
so that the prayers are once again being said,
and shared vision will once again guide us.

This time of trouble, this darkness
which at times, seems even to blot out
the golden sun's light,
will end
as the Christ Spirit and Divine Mother
awaken in our hearts,
and the Sun's golden rays stream out
to bathe and infuse all of us
and everything with light!

## **Look at the Sun/Change Within** by JahSun

Look at the sun begin to rise
Over the green rolling hills I'm lucky to be alive

Feel the warmth beat down unto my eyes
As the dark turns to day see the colors by my side

And I feel, something happening
Yes I feel, a change within

See the sun in the sky
And watch the birds as they fly by
See the light shining through the trees
As I sit back and wonder, what it means to me

And I feel, something happening
Yes I feel, a change within

Watch the sun in the west
Its been a long hard day and I've tried to do my best
See the sun sinking low
Beneath the watery waves tells me its my time to go

Still I feel, something happening
Yes I feel, a change within

## Life Is a Game

At the House of cards----

You can...
Take a chance
Roll the dice
Find true love.

Play the game of Life
on the Earth board.

Level Up!

Live, Learn and Love.

## **This Wonderful Thing** by Allyson Ditto

As mysterious as it is,
It comes and goes,
We try our hardest,
But we never know,
Which way we'll go,
We have to stay with it,
Because you never know,
How you'll end up,
Or which way you'll turn,
As time flies by,
You still learn,
New and amazing things,
That this wonderful thing gives,
Each day we go on,
But we know we can't live,
Without this wonderful thing,
That comes from above,
This wonderful thing,
This thing we call love.

## Love Is by Jennifer H.

Love is freedom
never pushing over me
only holding me steady,
as I tread these murky waters.
Gently lifting me when I feel down

Slowly caressing the fear and pain
till it loosens it's grip and leaves
my body

Love is Pure never telling me who to be
only showing me what I can be,
and how to get there

Love never pulls or pushes me
wanting me to feel low
to the ground

Love builds me up, wanting
me to be, all that I can be

Guiding me forward
shining a light so bright
all that is not right
for me dissolves away

## **Replenishing** by Jennifer H.

Sitting silent in the woods
a gentle breeze brushes by your face
its not the wind
the trees are breathing all around you

Breathing life into the world,
          Replenishing

Standing, silently, crying against a trunk
-sweet release, ease the energy out

Trees

Soaking in your tears, your fears
Holding space for all your pain
with nothing to gain

But a song, of love and gratitude
          Replenishing
Necessary.

For the space they hold
for us all

Standing tall
beacons of energy

Anchoring in reality

Shifting the winds

Swirling the world
into
Peace and balance.

## **Meeting** by Robin Houghton

Meeting a stranger
I feel trees dancing
--together but upright--
dancing together but alone:
Branches brush
leaves entwine
roots tip-toe-touch
in the
D~
e D
e a
e r
p k~
Who knows why
the forest grows as it does:
Which friends stand together
--strong through centuries of wax & wane,
of wind & rain--
Which fall away
--too long lost in another's shadow,
too little time
dancing
in Sun's embrace...

## **Daughters** by Anonymous

Mothers and daughters like prickly roses,
sweet smelling, a temporary joy.
A mother's womb--once sacred and warm.
Who have you become, this child of mine?

Sweet smelling, a temporary joy.
Wear your gloves, protect your heart.
Who have you become, this child of mine?
Silence, searching, empty space.

Wear your gloves, protect your heart.
A garden that takes much work.
Silence, searching, empty space.
Words that shatter, crack and tear.

A garden that takes much work.
A mother's womb--once sacred and warm.
Words that shatter, crack and tear.
Mothers and daughters like prickly roses.

## A year in Venango

The tornado---
Running thru sheets of rain
Sirens going off
carrying my toddler in her cloth diaper
to my neighbor's basement--
the older kids didn't like the
dark, musty smell, dirt floor and cobwebs.
No lights, chairs or food.
We huddled together.

The car wreck---
over drinking
a gallon of wine--
my car in the field with a cow--
A strange beautiful woman
wearing a suede dress with beads
gave me a ride.
(White Buffalo Calf Woman)
Vomit
on her back seat.
I don't know how I got to my friend's
who lived next door.
Every cell in my body is sick.
I have alcohol poisoning---
I don't remember what happened to my car.
I vow never to over drink again.

The hospitals---
I remember my son being hospitalized
he couldn't breath.
"We have new techniques for dealing with asthma."
the steroid induced psychosis and paranoia---
he thought his roommate was trying to kill him.
I checked him out of the hospital
and was reported to CYS (Children & Youth Services)

At home,
he threw his burger on the wall
claiming that it was poison
I watched it smear down to the floor.

Another time--
his childhood friend, hit him with a chair
he had to have his head put back together--
like Humpty Dumpty--
the big metal staples
like a carpenters gun.

My daughter--
had a close call too,
allergic reaction to an immunization
led to fever and convulsions---
we rode in the ambulance that time.

The eviction---
My downstairs neighbor
and landlord's daughter
said we were too much trouble.

The collapse---
I remember
giving up custody of my two youngest daughters--
one, only a month old.
They went to stay with their dad
while I 'visited' 3rd North--
the place at the hospital
with a locked door at the entrance
and rooms for talking, resting and art.

When released--
I had two children instead of four
and I moved away
from Venango.

**Child**

Grandmothers are there for you
when
mothers are busy--
with the business of living,

working, taking care of the younger children,
cooking dinner, partying, playing bingo and
other important things.

When I was in the hospital
recovering from a suicide attempt---
It was my grandmother
that came to see me.

Poor mom--
she really didn't have a clue.

My mother---
often so busy
keeping busy--
that life passed by.

She was not there when I needed her---
there is an empty,
painful place
that will not be filled.

It's sad when parents
don't give their children
the love and support,
they need
But,
We can.
Love ourselves--
the inner child
who feels sad--

Give her
the support, attention and love
that she deserves.

## Reminiscent

How many can remember a family Homestead?

Dirt Basement
Jars of beans, corn and tomatoes.

Thin slices,
sweet pickles
in a crock.

Sugar cookies as big as pancakes,
under the sink,
In a big metal pan.

Walks thru the wet dew
to pick the morning bouquet---
Grandma putting on galoshes over her shoes--
She always wore a dress,
tending to the garden, the rabbits, the yard.

The dinner meal was
Noon,
Every day.

Desert was a big honeycomb,
dripping...
                golden syrup.

In the sitting room,
there were violets,
of different hues.

Grandpa would fall asleep
in his evening chair
with the news on.

Tractors, kitties and 4-leaf clovers.

The screened-In porch,
we'd sit together,
I'd swing,
her mother, didn't say much,
hands always busy,
crocheting.

When i hugged her,
the hearing aid
made a ringing sound.

## Childhood Smoke

Are we like the flowers---
beautiful,
fragile yet strong
at the same time?
As we get older,
does the world get colder?
Like a song,
that passes too quickly?

When your mother tells you that your dad doesn't love you---
When your step-dad kicks your cat and tells you how good you look----
When you can't breathe
because of all the cigarette butts laying around---
Its
Childhood Smoke.

I remember chasing wild kittens in my Grandma's barn.
I found a 4-leaf clover that day,
and I knew all would be well.

Please, Please Momma,
don't drive so fast.

I gave my mom a hard time,
Coming,
After 3 days of labor---
Out I came, feet first---
It was like,
I knew what I was in for,
And, I had changed my mind.

The story is that my mom
threw me, as a newborn,
Perhaps I just slipped off the couch---
But my grandmother took care of me.
She was an angel,

Who now, still helps me
from her place, on the other side.

One day, my mom packed up my stuff
and dropped me off
at my dad's house---
soon after,
I woke up with his hands around my throat---

I don't know what's worse---
Not being loved by my dad---
Or being loved too much by my stepdad.

I grew up watching Gilligen's Island---
If those seven strangers could get along
on a deserted island,
then why couldn't we?

Round and Round, we go.
For a three hour tour, we go.

Where is the love and light?
We are.
We create,
by living our lives.
In fact, that is why we are here.
We are one,
of the many threads,
in this tapestry of life.

Look back to that 4-leaf clover,
We are never alone, and
We are loved.

The angels are singing---
Look at that Cheryl---
She took Childhood Smoke,
and turned it into Light.

## Begin Again

They say we are a product of our childhood.

I say...
Break the cycle.
Change the story.
Turn the page.
Start a new day.
Begin again!
Move out
of judgment.
Starting over is Fun!

In the 80's...
I graduated high school, learned about computers and became a mother.

It did not matter to me
that
They called me a single mother,
and other things.

I was happy---I had someone to unconditionally love.
It would never be the same.
I had been searching for something all my life,
and I found it.
It was a divine responsibility.
That little being gave me his trust.
He also came to teach me---
living, loving, giving.

In the 90's...
I began the 3rd decade
of my life.
Had 4 children
Married
Divorced

Left my hometown
Went to college
and
Married again.
I was busy.

Y2K...
the years started over.

When I turned 40...
I got my first tattoo, my college diploma and moved across the country.
I rode on the back of a motorcycle,
touring the badlands.

Starting over is fun.

The year I turned 50...
I had my natal chart done
and visited
Mount Shasta
for the first time.

Some serious seeds
were planted
on that trip.

I was on my spiritual path,
following the trail of bread crumbs.

Three years later,
Star Knowledge
happened to me.

I was 53
according to Mayan belief---
starting a new spin
of my life
here on Earth.

When I turned 55
I had a plan
to 'check out' of this Earth hotel
(You can check out but you can never leave)

Instead,
Went to Maui
spoke at the
Temple of Peace
on the 12/12 portal.

Begin again.
I left home, hearth and an unhealthy relationship.

Don't Look Back!

My tears joined
the saltwater
of my sister, Ocean
and
the sea turtles held space for me.

I worked, made friends and went to women's circles again.
Settled in routine.

Then,
I got the message---
"Come to Mount Shasta"
Here
I Am.

Starting over is fun.
After all,
Life is an adventure.

## What Now?

Don't fight it---
you'll only sink
Quicker--
Quicksand.

Up a creek
without a paddle--

Down a narrow, winding
road---
No room to turn
Around.

What now?

I am lost
in the maze of life.

Reached a dead end---
At the Final stop sign.

What now?

The tide is high---
"Just keep swimming."
Stay above water.
Grab a life line, preserver or
anchor.

This board called
Life--
is changing---
                    sliding---
          into something
else.

What now?

Shut your eyes---
Be still---
Calm,
Center---

The answer you are seeking
is within.
"You've had it all along."

**123456798** **by Cody Ray Richardson**

In pitch black of the dark night of the soul.
Treading in a sea of tears.
I turn on my back in rest.
Still kicking like an upset child on the floor.
The stars admit light from the past.
So bright yet most dead supposedly.
May or may not be it truth.
Still they entertain hope.
So far away yet brilliant.
Like a deer in the headlights.
Struck by some kind of way out.
To go in any further in Is to arrive in the outer.
123 456 789 the 8 should clearly be where the 9 is.
Those mischievous tyrants have turned us all on ourselves.
Cowards fighting through deception.
The heart is a compass.
Follow its rhythm like a metronome.
Change your tune.
You are your composer.

## Faith

None will escape
this mortal coil---

sooo
might as well
greet your yin.

If you disagree
with a decision--
another chance
will come around.

Don't worry.
Have faith.

Be like owl,
sit back,
take it all in--
then *make your move.*

Move
and let life happen.

## Listen

Dorothy takes flight--

Alice tumbles--

Whole worlds exist
in the strangest places--
like on a dandelion bloom.

If you listen carefully,
you will hear them.

The Walrus recites poetry,
and a rabbit keeps time.

Plants are always watching--
they witness--
our ups and downs,
our dramas.

You can talk to them--
If they like you
they will talk back.

Listen.
Be like Horton,
Who do you hear?

## Breath of Imagination

A red and gold lizard
came to me--
he said
        "Take a toke. Majik dust--
        Drink the gold. Spice up your life."

and shared
        "I used to be a fish stuck in a pond."

Take it up a notch.
Move up the scale--
Bass, Alto or Soprano?
What tone are you?

Stretch
        a little higher.
Stuck?

Rock that boat--
gently, calmly. It's safe.
Make your move--

Change.

## A Message

Every day is a different reality---

Yesterday's events
matter not.

It's all a hologram anyway--

So you don't need to be concerned--
Try to fix anyone--

Tomorrow
we'll all be awash
in an ocean
of sunlight.

Just be kind,
the rest will work itself out.

## What If I Told You
**by Giovanna Taormina**

What if I told you that serenity is green?

And that blessings are fresh with flavor?

Would you agree?

What if I told you
that sunshine is a bowl of cool icecream?

And flavors are jumping with appreciation?

Would you believe me?

Would you frown if I served you
fruit that is brown?

Or hamburger stuffed with rocks and grass?

Would you still feel my heartfelt spirit?

Can you please join me in my childlike truth?

Throw your life, money and inheritance on the floor?

Feel the light uplifting stillness--

Amore, Madre, dogs and peace!

## **The Blind Princess** by Shambala

Once upon a time in a magical land, there was a king who had three daughters. The youngest who an aura of radiant kindness and beauty, was also blind. Each morning she loved to slowly meander through the garden listening to the birds sing, the fountains flow, and the springs gurgle. She would smell and touch the flowers enchanted and intoxicated by the buzzing of the bees.

Her two sisters sometimes made fun of her, saying there would be no suitor who would care to have a blind bat. She would go to her room and cry. But still she was mostly happy, accepting her fate, knowing that all things have a divine purpose.

One day the King who was a very kind ruler, called his Wizard in for a chat and asked him to please think for a few days about his beautiful blind daughter who had a heart of gold.

So the Wizard went up on the holy mountain and sat silently in the wilderness for a few days, when a vision came to him. He saw a regal prince riding up on a precious Palomino pony and falling in love with the blind princess. So he returned to the castle and told his vision to the king.

Soon when it was time for the Harvest Festival, people were invited from all parts of the Kingdom. They prepared the large public park and square for the gay celebratory festivities and feasts in order to Give Thanks to Father Sun and Mother Earth for all the abundance. When the day arrived people were pouring in from all parts of the kingdom bringing gifts and a harvest cornucopia clad in their finest apparel. And sure enough, just as the wizard had seen in his vision, there approached a handsome prince on a Palomino horse. He entered the sporting contests contests such as jousting, fencing, and riding and won them all.

The King, good to his word, which was that the winner could ask and seek  the hand of the princess daughter of his choice. Thus he said to the prince " please choose which of the maidens you choose to marry". The two older ones immediately made themselves known near the king with smiles and coy looks flashing their eyelashes all the while. But the prince asked the king where was the other daughter, he heard there was three of them. The two daughters that were present tried to dismiss the question, but the king being very honest sent for his youngest daughter, the blind princess.

The Prince upon seeing her, his heart was fast smitten with the arrow of pure Love. Thus he chose her. The two other princesses were angry but his mind was made. The blind  princess too felt overjoyed and a warm tingling flushed all throughout her body and being.

She stutteringly gladly accepted the prince's proposal and the crowd let out a great cheer. The wedding date was set for the first day of spring which happened to be a Saturday. Everyday now the princess would sit in the royal garden excited with anticipation.

When the time of the Betrothal finally arrived and all things were in preparation. The musicians began to play and people showered confetti from all the balconies. They rode in great procession to the Cathedral. When they were pronounced husband and wife the prince kissed her fully and deeply on the lips, setting off a flash of incredible light and her eyes were opened and she could see. They rode off into a majestic sunset pulled in a golden carriage by four white horses feeling the sweetest nuptial bliss and lived Happily Ever After in service to everyone in the Kingdom.

***This story is dedicated to my daughter Maia Starla Prem-Blossom.***

## All The Things Money Can't Buy
**by Benjamin B. Brown**

Everyone says they want it,
Everyone says they need it.
But what everyone doesn't know
Is that you can't own it.
Because it owns you.
It owns your mind, body and your soul.
Some people do crazy things to get it.
Because they think it's the only thing
that can bring them happiness.
But they don't know.

My parents put the pressure on me.
They have it and no one doubts that.
Three big cars and a pool in the back.
But does it make them happy?
Does it set them free? No.
It forces them to do crazy things
and put pressure on me.
"What if you are dirt poor?"
"What if you have no dough?"
"That's okay," I say. Because I know.
The people with bills are empty inside
and their fake smiles are all for show.

## Life is What You Make It

Can't fall asleep---
while the god of thunder
is pounding.

What a grave gambit.
Will the true Oz
Please stand Up--
Please stand Up?

Clap! Yay!
Another day--
another argument averted.
A sacred rite
saves the day.
The Way of the dove--
Peace Ritual.
It starts as a feeling---
becomes a knowing--
deep in your bones.

Who gets your praise?
Do you believe in the one true god?
You and I are God--
it's only hidden
in plain sight.

Feeling stress?
Take it down a notch--
There is no lien on this life--
only what you give up.
You can bank on that.

"No worries".
Play like children.
Have fun.
Party at my house!

## You Tell On Yourself
**by Nicole Cunningham**

You tell on yourself by the friends you seek.
By the very manner in which you speak.
By the way you employ your leisure time.
By the use you make of your dollar and dime.

You tell who you are by the things you wear.
By the spirit in which your burdens you bear.
By the kind of things at which you laugh.
By the records you play on the phonograph.

You tell who you are by the way you walk.
By the things of which you delight to talk.
By the manner in which you bear defeat.
By so simple a thing as how you eat.

By the books you choose from the well-filled shelf.
In these ways and more you tell on yourself.
So there's really no particle of sense.
In an effort to keep up false pretense.

## **Show Me Truth** by JahSun

While we're in this world
What you gonna do?
You can let the rainclouds burst, or let the sun shine through
Its up to you

Will you show me, will you show me some Truth?
Will you show me, before you let me loose?

While we're in this Life
How will you make your mark?
Will you do a sacred dance?
Make your life a work of art?

Will you show me, will you show me some Truth?
Will you show me, before you let me loose?

You can cuss and moan
And see what that might do
Or choose to look inside
And seek the answer within you

Will you show me, will you show me some Truth?
Will you show me, before you let me loose?

## So Sweet
### by Robin Houghton

Dancing, dancing-is so Sweet
In the Blood and Out the Feet
Be a Wave in rhythmic Ocean
Let the Body show Devotion
Prancing, spinning in that Flow
Witness thoughts & feelings Go
Weaving, winding Round 'n Round
Both upright-and on the Ground
Contact Improv with some Friends
Find new ways your body Bends
Dancing chaos, dancing Love
Up from Earth, down from Above
Meditation-in a Trance
What is Life but one big DANCE ?!

## Looking Back
**by Caroline Rice**

I look back on my life,
Thinking what I have done.
What things have I taken for granted?
What things have I done for fun?

It's a weary road I travel,
With many shortcomings.
But the moments of happiness,
Are the most important things.

I look back down this road,
And see mistakes I've made.
Yes, I've made bad choices,
And their price I have paid.

I have fallen many times,
Just about given up,
But friends, family, and the Lord
Were there to help me up.

Even though my steps wander,
Off my path from time to time,
That's just because I tried new things,
Sometimes spent every dime.

I can barely wait what's ahead for me,
And where my path will lead.
Each step is a grain of sand,
A grain of sand I need.

## **FAUCET by Jan Dorrell**

Sirens, car horns, metal against metal.
Scurrying crowds crossing the street.
Babies crying, men swearing, cat calls
Construction noise

Faucet

How am I?
I've not been well at all.
My sciatica is acting up, I can hardly walk.
Plantar fasciitis makes it impossible to wear normal shoes.
Dr. says my blood pressure is dangerously high and my breathing is labored.
My teeth ache, my hair is falling out, and my eyesight gets worse every day.
Other than that.....

Faucet

Children today are ungrateful.
My kids were spoiled, but it's over the top with my grandchildren.
They have no work ethic, no manners, no sense of responsibility.
Just tragic!
Oh, did I show you Josh's baseball picture?
He was MVP in the league.
Amy was homecoming queen and her boyfriend is Dr. Sander's son.
Her 4.32 GPA is going to land her multiple scholarships and college acceptances.

Faucet

Our country is going down the tubes.
Have you seen the cost of eggs?
They used to be a responsible substitute for a meal or two.
Not any more!!
Don't get me started on gas prices
They keep me from leaving town.
When I was a kid, a nickel got 5 penny candies.
Someone is lining their pockets at the expense of all of us.

Faucet

My new health regiment is just amazing.
I've eliminated all carbs and eat nothing but broccoli, celery and chicken wings.
4 hours of exercise a day keeps me from thinking about food.
Have you kept up with the latest supplements for optimal health, weight loss,
electrolyte balance, a radiant smile, and sure fire man magnetic force?
Let's have lunch every day for the next month so I can share what I've learned.

Faucet

I bought the most adorable Gucci swimsuit for the summer. A steal at $550.
Then Asher insisted I get the $480 Celine Edge sunglasses to complete my beachwear.
My closet is filled with fashionable attire.
My daughter is a mini me. Guess Jeans are her favorite right now.
NO ONE she knows owns a pair of Levis.
Shey'd be laughed out of school.
Did I tell you my sister-in-law's cousin is getting married?
She has to buy her dress off the rack.
How embarrassing!!!
By the way, who are you wearing?

Faucet

Some one, please, turn off the tap!!!!

## (H)Ash Sunday

The more gentle you are with life---
the more gentle life is with you.

What are you willing to give up?

How about the need to be right?

How about that righteous anger---
I have a right--
They were wrong.

Waiting for an apology
that will never come.

I'm right, I know better--
says Pooh's Rabbit.

Do you have honey?
Then be happy. Hash?
Even better.

The way of Pooh--
Don't be bothered.

If its a bother--
just leave it.

Let it Be.

## Life

Life is a Road we all travel--
Often there are detours, construction work
or potholes.

There is always more
than one route to take--

Sometimes we take the fast lane--
other times we go the long way, scenic route.

There are days our vehicle
needs a jumpstart or a fluid change.

When there's bad weather--
we can 'stay in'
Or,
if we feel out-of-line,
get an alignment.

Some trips require advance planning,
while others,
just hop in and go.

How do you travel on your road?

Are you cautious--wear your seatbelt?
Or are you a risk-taker,
Jump first, ask questions later?

Are you like the hare,
in a hurry to get there--
or like the tortoise--
slow and steady wins the race?

Either way--
the choice is yours to make.
We will all reach the finish line--
end of the road,
when it is time.
So, might as well enjoy the journey.

"Life is a highway and I'm gonna ride it all night long."

About the author---

Cheryl Lunar Wind lives in the Mount Shasta area in a little town called Weed. She is a practitioner of Mayan cosmology, Lakota ceremony, Star Knowledge and the Universal Laws including the Law of One. Her hobbies are writing poetry, music, dance, drum circles and love for all life; plant, animal and crystal. Cheryl has been a guide and spiritual teacher for many years. Now she shares wisdom and wit through poetry, and has published poetry books; Know Your Way, We Are One, Follow the White Rabbit, Love Your Light and now LIFE: Shared thru Poetry.

Testimonials---

"A rare collection filled with raw, courageous honesty. Thought-provoking words that will stop you in your tracks."
Snow Thorner, ED Open Sky Gallery, Montague, California

"Cheryl's poetry is very inspiring--particularly the way she compares life with the forces of nature. There is a special element in her poems that opens my heart and fills my soul with divine possi-bilities."
Giovanna Taormina, Co-Founder, One Circle Foundation

"Cheryl's poems have helped me to uncover and honor my own hidden memories. The beauty of her spirit is evident in each tender, insightful passage."
Marguerite Lorimer, www.earthalive.com

www.ingramcontent.com/pod-product-compliance
Lightning Source LLC
LaVergne TN
LVHW010544100826
845148LV00013B/2599